Wild Weather

Written by
Jill Atkins

There are many different kinds of wild weather. Many of these are caused by the wind.

A **hurricane** is a colossal storm that begins in the sea in tropical parts of the planet.

The wind gets stronger as it spins around and travels across the sea.

This is a hurricane seen from high in the sky.

The wind is strongest on the outside of the whirl, but there is not much wind in the eye of the storm.

If a strong hurricane hits land it could smash homes and blow down trees.

It could make such big waves it would swamp the land.

Some people could be wounded or made homeless.

A **typhoon** is similar to a hurricane.

A **tornado** is different from a hurricane.

It is a cloud like a funnel that travels over land instead of over the sea. It is often called a **twister** because it whirls so fast.

People should find shelter underground if they can.

A tornado is so strong it could lift rocks and boulders.

It could flatten wooden homes in a few seconds.

A **monsoon** blows from cold parts of the planet to hot parts.

It brings colossal amounts of rain. The streets could fill with water.

Can you see? This boy's flip flops are floating in the water!

There is a different kind of wild weather in hot, dry lands where there isn't any rain.

In a desert in North Africa, a strong wind could make a **sandstorm**. It looks like a cliff in the sky. People could get sand in their eyes!

Sometimes, a sandstorm might blow a dust cloud far into different lands.

This drawing shows the pyramids in a sandstorm, hundreds of years ago.

Would you like to be in a sandstorm?

In lands such as Alaska and Canada, it could be colder than in a freezer!

It might be so cold that someone's eyelashes could snap off!

There could be extreme cold, where you could freeze to death if you were not dressed in thick coats.

This group of people are dressed well for the snow.

In these cold lands, you might need sunglasses because the white snow is so bright.

Or you could be out in a **blizzard**.

Thick snow would be blown in the wind and could make deep snow drifts.

People would need to clear roads if they wanted to travel.

Many lands might have wind, rain, thunder and lightning, hail, sleet and snow, but not all of them have wild weather.